How to Set Prices
in a Service Business

A Step by Step Guide to
Pricing Your Services

By Meir Liraz

Published by BizMove
www.bizmove.com

Table of Contents

MEIR LIRAZ

1. Introduction

This guide discusses costing and setting prices of services to assure that each job earns a reasonable profit. The figures used in the tables and examples do not reflect what your service costs, set prices, and profits actually would or should be. The figures are used to demonstrate costing and set prices and are rounded off for further simplicity. Because of the importance and sometimes complexity of costing and pricing, it is good business practice to consult your trade association and particularly your accountant to learn what are the best current practices, cost ratios, and profit margins in your service business.

2. Setting Prices Problems

Many businesses are not making a profit today because they do not know the basic concepts of costing and set prices. The situation is most serious in the service business because each service performed has a different cost. Frequently, the service business must bid for jobs by making a price quotation in competition with similar businesses. Can you calculate your costs for your service and quote a price that is competitive and returns a profit?

Without realizing what they are doing, some business owners set their selling price below their total cost. This may result in more business for the company, but a loss will be incurred on each sale. Occasionally, a business owner who lacks a knowledge of costing will try to compensate by setting prices very high. The end result is that the business is not price competitive and does not attract sufficient customers to survive. Frequently, a business earns a profit on some particular service and loses money on other services without knowing which services are earning a profit and which services are incurring a loss. The year-end income statement combines the profits and losses from the various services performed over the year. Therefore, it is impossible to determine the profitability of specific service jobs from a year-end income statement.

Use a simplified approach to cost accounting that reflects the needs of the business and reports the cost with a reasonable degree of accuracy. The total cost of producing any service is composed of three parts: 1) the material cost, 2) the labor cost, and 3) the overhead cost. Direct materials and direct labor + overhead = total cost of service.

3. Cost Determination

Direct Material Cost

The direct material cost is made up of the cost to you for parts and supplies that are used on specific jobs. Once the list of parts and supplies to be used is developed, a check with the supplier will give an up-to-date material cost. The shipping and other handling (storage etc.) costs for the parts should be included in the material cost.

Direct Labor Cost

The direct labor costs include those labor costs identified with a specific service job. The labor cost involved in providing a service is determined by multiplying the number of direct labor hours required by the cost per direct labor hour. It is very important to determine accurately the amount of direct labor hours involved to complete the service; therefore, you must use a time clock, worksheet, or a daily time card for each employee to determine the exact amount of labor time spent on each service job.

The hourly cost of direct labor can be figured (priced) two ways. One it can be the hourly wage only, with fringe benefits, Social Security, Workers' Compensation, etc., (all labor-related costs) allocated to overhead. Or two, the hourly direct labor cost can include the hourly wage plus the employer's contribution to Social Security, unemployment compensation, disability, holidays and vacations, hospitalization and other fringe benefits (payroll costs).

By this second method, the added payroll costs for vacations, holidays and benefits are expressed as percentages of direct hourly wages. For instance, if two weeks of vacation and ten holidays are given annually, this amounts to four weeks per year or 7.7% (i.e., four weeks off divided by fifty-two weeks $4 : 52 = 7.7\%$) of total labor cost was for time off. Thus, to determine the total direct labor cost per hour by this method, you must add the prorated cost of the payroll taxes, worker's compensation, holidays and vacation pay, hospitalization, etc., to the hourly wage paid. As a rule of thumb, the sum of the various payroll-benefit costs have generally been in the range of 20% to 30% of the hourly wages paid. It is more complicated to figure but more precise to use the higher labor cost (including labor related labor costs). The following table shows a sample calculation for figuring the total direct labor cost using this more exact method.

ABC Repair Company

Table 1: Direct Labor Cost Calculation

(1) Hourly Wage	(2) Payroll Taxes @12%	(3) Workers Compensation @3%	(4) Total Direct Labor Cost Per Year*	(5) Vacation and Holiday Cost per Working Hour**	(6) Actual Direct Labor Cost per Working Hour***
8.04	.96	.24	19219.2	.57	9.87
9.78	1.17	.30	24400	.69	11.94
10.20	1.23	.30	24398.4	.72	12.45
10.86	1.29	.33	25958.4	.78	13.26
11.55	1.38	.36	27643.2	.84	14.13
12.30	1.47	.36	29390.4	.87	15.00
		Total	150,009.6		

*40 hrs/wk x 52 wks/yr = 2080 hrs/yr

**6.25% of Columns 1 + 2 + 3.

***Columns 1 + 2 + 3 + 5.

Overhead Cost

Overhead includes all job related costs other than direct materials and direct labor. Your overhead cost depends on which of the two ways you figured direct labor costs, with or without the labor-related payroll-benefits costs. If you did not include these expenses in direct labor, then you must include them in overhead. In our examples, however, these labor-related costs are included in direct labor and not in overhead. Either way the effect on the total job cost is the same, but your overhead cost varies accordingly.

Because they may not know how to allocate (or assign) overhead costs to the services performed, many business owner-managers miscalculate or avoid considering overhead costs.

Overhead is the indirect cost of the service and is made up of indirect materials, indirect labor, and other indirect costs related to particular services. Indirect materials are too minor to include as direct material costs. Incidental supplies and machine lubricants are examples. Indirect labor is the wages, salaries, and other payroll-benefit costs incurred by workers who do not perform the service but who support the main service function, such as, clerical, supply, and janitorial employees. Other costs, like taxes, depreciation, insurance, and transportation are also part of the overhead cost because the service cost includes a portion of all indirect costs (overhead). The following table projects total overhead for all services for one year. To figure the portion of overhead related to particular services or jobs, you allocate the various overhead costs by calculating the overhead rate.

The way you calculate the overhead rate should relate the overhead costs to the primary cause for the overhead cost being expended, reflecting a reasonable amount of total overhead to each service. The overhead rate can be expressed as a decimal, as a percentage, or as an hourly rate. The use of the overhead rate helps to assure that all the overhead costs expended throughout the year will be recovered as the business's services are sold throughout the year.

In a situation where employee wages vary a lot, as when higher paid employees work with more expensive equipment, the overhead cost is allocated on the basis of direct labor cost. This occurs because a large proportion of the overhead cost will consist of equipment depreciation (other indirect cost), interest on the capital invested in equipment, and electrical costs. The overhead rate is determined as follows:

(1) Overhead Rate =

$$\frac{\text{Total Overhead Cost}}{\text{Total Direct Labor Cost}}$$

This is the most common method for allocating overhead cost to the specific service performed. The above rate is suitable for machine shops and auto repair shops.

In some cases there is relatively little difference in the hourly wages paid to different employees. In other cases, no relationship exists between the level of the worker's skill and the amount of equipment used by the worker. Under such circumstances, total overhead cost may be allocated on the basis of direct labor hours as follows:

(2) Overhead Rate =

$$\text{Overhead Rate} = \frac{\text{Total Overhead Cost}}{\text{Total Direct Labor Hours}}$$

The above rate is suitable for businesses such as secretarial services or janitorial services. The overhead costs result mainly from the workspace, supervision, and electricity that the workers need in order to provide the service. Using formula (2), it is possible to determine the overhead cost per hour per employee.

Calculating the Overhead Cost

In determining the total overhead cost, a business should not depend solely on last year's income statement. Due to inflation and business growth, last year's overhead costs do not accurately reflect today's overhead cost. The best approach is to project the overhead costs for the near future, that is, the anticipated overhead expenses for the next six months to one year. The projected overhead cost will reflect additional administrative salaries, the depreciation of new equipment that the business plans to purchase, rent increases, energy cost increases, etc. Table 2 shows projected overhead expenses for a business, ABC Repair Company.

The payroll taxes included in the projected overhead expenses for the service business are only those paid on executive and office salaries. The direct labor payroll, taxes, holiday pay, vacation pay etc., are included in the direct labor cost shown in Table 1.

ABC Repair Company

Table 2: Projected Overhead Expenses for the upcoming year

Indirect Materials

Office Expenses	1,800
Postage	450
Repairs	2,900
Shop Supplies	2,700
Utilities	2,400
Telephone	4,400
	14,650

Indirect Labor

Executive Salaries	30,000
Office Salaries	7,000
Payroll Taxes	12,000
Travel & Entertainment	700
	49,700

Other Indirect Costs

Accounting	2,400
Advertising	4,800
Auto-Truck Expense	5,400
Depreciation	9,650
Insurance	1,240
Interest	2,560
Licenses	650
Miscellaneous Expense	500
Rent	8,450
	35,650

Total Overhead	100,000

To ensure that all overhead costs are included, it is best to project the overhead costs for a full fiscal year. This aids in the treatment of expenses that occur only once each year, such as business licenses.

4. Cost Calculation Example

Perhaps the most common type of service business is the repair business. The cost calculation procedure illustrated here for the repair business can be used for other types of service businesses. The only precaution that needs to be taken is that the appropriate overhead rate formula which reflects the business's operation, as discussed above, be used in the calculation.

It has been estimated, based upon previous experience, that a specific repair job will require $20 of parts and 2 hours of labor by an employee whose labor cost is $5.00 per hour. (These estimates will be used throughout this Guide.) As discussed earlier, the total cost of producing any service is composed of: 1) the material cost, 2) the labor cost, and 3) the overhead cost.

To determine the material cost (the cost of the parts), check the cost of the part in your inventory or get a price quote from your parts suppliers. A parts wholesaler is the source of the $20 material cost in this example.

To determine the total direct labor cost, the number of hours of direct labor used is multiplied by the actual direct labor cost per hour. An employee whose actual direct labor cost is $5.00 per hour, including payroll taxes and fringe benefits (see

Table 1), requires two hours to complete the repair job.

Labor Cost = Direct Labor Cost per Hour x Hours Required

Labor Cost = $5.00 per Hour x 2 Hours

Labor Cost = $10.00

The projected overhead expenses were projected to be $100,000 per year, as shown in Table 2. The nature of the repair business is that overhead costs are most directly related to direct labor costs than to direct material costs. The total projected direct labor cost including payroll taxes and fringe benefits was determined to be $50,003.20 (see Table 1). The formula selected to determine the overhead rate bases upon the direct labor cost is:

(1) Overhead Rate =

Total Overhead Cost

Total Direct Labor Cost:

$100,000 : $50,003.20 = 2.00

In most small to medium businesses, the overhead rate is between one and two (i.e., between 100% and 200% of the direct labor cost). Businesses that are very labor intensive, such as a janitorial service, will have an overhead rate much less that 100%

To determine the overhead cost allocated to a specific job, the labor cost is multiplied by the overhead rate as shown below.

(1) Overhead Cost = Direct Labor Cost x Overhead Rate

$10.00 x 2.00 = $20.00

To determine the total cost of the repair job, the material cost, the direct labor cost, and the overhead cost are added together:

Material Cost	20.00
Direct Labor Cost	10.00
Overhead Cost	20.00
	Total 50.00

5. How to Set Optimal Prices

Calculate the profit and add it to the total cost to get the price to charge for the service, in this case a repair job. Prices charged by competitors (similar service businesses), economic conditions of supply and demand, and legal, political, and consumer pressures all influence the profit you can expect for your service and hence the price you can charge for your jobs. Inflation, the amount of business you have (i.e., number of jobs), and your productivity (the efficiency and quality of your business and service) also all effect your profit and the way you figure your prices. You can choose from several pricing methods. Common business practice is to express profit as a percentage of the base used for pricing calculations no matter which pricing method you use.

Set Prices Alternatives

In considering the total cost of the repair job discussed above, the material cost can normally be predicted with a high degree of accuracy. Labor and overhead costs cannot be predicted with such a high degree of accuracy. An employee may not feel well on a given day. Or there may be an equipment breakdown. Either will result in higher than expected labor costs. A provision to adjust for fluctuating labor and overhead costs can be established through your approach to profit. The profit can be applied to the three costs independently, allowing for variations in labor and overhead costs among jobs. For example, a 10% profit on material, a 30% profit on direct labor, and a 30% profit on overhead can be used to determine the price of the service.

Material Cost + Profit of Material		
$20 +	$20 x 10%= $22.00	$2
Direct Labor Cost + Profit on Direct Labor		
$10 +	$10 x 30% = $13.00	$3
Overhead Cost + Profit on Overhead		
$20 +	$20 x 30%= $26.00	$6
———	———	———
$50 Cost	$61.00 Price	$11 Profit

The concept of applying a different rate of profit on the three underlying costs (material, labor, and overhead) is one method of dealing with the large difference in predictability of costs that exists between labor and materials in most service businesses. To reflect the fluctuations in utilization and cost of labor and overhead from job to job, your profit on labor and overhead should normally be higher than profits on materials.

Direct Cost Pricing

With this method you set your selling price based on direct cost, that is, on direct materials (DM) and direct labor (DL). DM of $20 plus DL of $10 equals

Direct Costs of $30. Overhead (OH) costs are $20; so to earn the $11 profit you need, your selling price must be at least $31 above your direct cost to charge; divide direct costs into overhead plus needed profit:

$31 ($11 + $20) : $30 = 103 1/3%

(proof $30 x 103 1/3% = $30 x 1.033 = $11)

In most small businesses, there is not a large amount of overhead cost associated with obtaining parts besides a telephone call to order them. Charging a large amount of overhead to parts may result in pricing yourself out of the market.

By all these methods you are deriving a selling price for your service. Sometimes however you start with the selling price already established - by competition or economic conditions. Then you must figure out the most cost you can incur and still earn your needed profit.

Setting Prices - Summary

The total cost of producing a service is composed of direct material, direct labor, and overhead costs. This cost information is used as a basis for setting prices and profit. From alternative pricing methods you select one that earns a satisfactory profit and is easy for you to use. Given regulations, competition, and the economy, you must have a pricing strategy that keeps your service competitive and profitable. The more exactly you figure your costs and set prices, the greater your chances for continued and profitable business.

6. How to Raise Prices Without Losing Customers

Everyone has to increase their prices eventually. If you're fortunate your customers won't notice. But in a budget conscious economy, the chances are they will.

If you run a contract- or consulting-based business, it can be doubly difficult to raise your rates because you're going to have to be upfront about the changes, and in all likelihood negotiate a new contract.

So it all makes for a worrisome situation. However, done right, raising your prices should not alienate your customers – particularly if they value you and your services. Here are some tips for raising your prices without losing customers.

1. Have a Pricing Strategy

A pricing strategy is a well-thought out plan that helps you calculate the prices, rates, or fees associated with your products or services. This may be reviewed monthly, quarterly, or annually depending on market forces, wholesale prices, and other "cost-of-doing-business" expenses. This way you can make rate increases a regular part of your business instead of waiting until it's too late.

2. Change Your Pricing Structure

Changing how you package and price your product or service is a very common way of making more money from customers without a rate hike and without ruffling feathers. Here are some ways to do this:

* Cross-sell Your Services – "Would you like fries with that?" Cross-selling is an easy way to increase sales of related services and meet your customer's needs. For example, a spa business could tag on a range of manicure services to its menu of massage services at a packaged price.

* Tier Your Pricing – Offering multiple price points across your business is a great way to up-sell products and services without raising prices. The plan here is that the tempted consumer will opt for the higher end of the tier. For example, a coffee shop may offer the following options:

1. Cappuccino @ $1.50

2. Cappuccino with a Shot of Syrup @ $2.50

3. Cappuccino with a Shot of Syrup and Cream @ $3.50

The variations are tempting, the value is clearly advertised and the decision to spend more is ultimately in the hands of your customer. The same basic, middle, and premium tiers can also be used in among consulting businesses.

* Change How You Bill Your Time – If you are a consultant or provide any service that involves selling your time in blocks, think about switching how you package your time. Trying to increase your hourly rate can be tough, instead sell your time in different chunks at different rates:

2 hours @ $85 per hour

5 hours @ $75 per hour

10 hours @ $65 per hour

3. What about Consultants or Service-Based Businesses?

If you operate a service-based business or are a freelancer/consultant, consider putting a stake in the ground and raise your rates after you've reached a certain client threshold. Options include raising your rates each year for new customers or after every 5 or 10 new customers, depending on how many clients you have on the books.

In the case of existing customers, approach your client directly and expect to negotiate your rate hike. If you are 100% confident in the value of your services then it's likely that your clients are too and are fully expecting this. Provide a heads up – if you plan on raising your rates in the new year, engage the client in November – this gives them enough time to review your proposed rate, negotiate, and plan accordingly.

4. What if a Customer Balks at the Price Hike?

Everyone has a reason and a right to raise their prices. But be prepared for some push-back and get ready to explain your increase. Explain your price hike in terms of the added value you bring and highlight any investments you have made in yourself (such as training) or your business that justifies the investment.

Above all, expect to negotiate and use your pricing strategy to plan for this. Don't go in too high to start with, because an educated client will almost certainly reject your opening rate without discussion. Likewise, ask yourself how low are you willing to go? What is the ideal mid-point at which you'd be happy to accept a negotiated rate?

7. Calculating Hourly and Project-Based Pricing

If you're a consultant, freelancer or any business that charges by the hour, you are going to have to determine and continuously review your pricing structure. For example, do you charge by the hour? What's a reasonable rate to ask? Are you better off charging clients on a project basis?

Here are some tips for calculating your hourly and project rates and how to negotiate pricing with your client.

1 Determining Your Worth

Deciding what to charge clients is a balancing act between market factors, business costs, and the value you bring to your clients. Before you quote any work, ask yourself these questions:

What is the market rate for work like yours in your industry and location?

How experienced are you? Not just in your line of work, but as a business owner? Being good at a skill is one thing, but being able to manage deadlines, meet expectations and above all, being dependable, are essential qualities for freelancers and consultants.

What rate are you willing to accept and will it cover your costs?

2. Calculating an Hourly Rate

If you've been a salaried employee all your life, making the switch to self-employment requires a change of thinking. Some companies may be tempted to coerce you into a rate that reflects what they'd be willing to pay a salaried employee. But self-employment brings its costs and credit to you. Your rate should reflect this, as well as your expertise.

If you are used to being a salaried employee, here's a good rule of thumb to follow when determining an hourly rate:

Divide your former salary by 52 (work weeks); then divide that number by 40 (the number of work hours in a week). Then mark it up 25-30%.

Your mark-up covers both your value and experience, but also takes care of our business costs such as networking, selling, and other administration, not forgetting your self-employment tax obligations and healthcare insurance costs.

3. Calculating Project Rates

Many clients will prefer to manage their costs and ask for you to price your work as a fixed project fee. This can also work to your benefit, if you price it right. However, it can also work against you, especially if your client is new and the project scope creeps beyond your original expectations.

The best way to calculate project rates is to spend some time scoping out what you'll deliver. For example, if you are a freelance copywriter and a client wants you to price out a two-page white paper, use your knowledge of your own work methods and familiarity with the subject matter to structure your time commitment, for example:

•Research: 2 Hours

•Interview subject matter expert: 1 Hour

•Produce First Draft: 4 Hours

•Two rounds of edits: 2 Hours

Total: 9 Hours @ $x hourly rate = $x

Remember, you don't have to put this calculation in front of your client, but it gives you a useful framework for covering your costs and delivering within scope. Don't forget to add a caveat to address that any work done over and above this scope of work will be charged at an hourly rate

4. Negotiating Your Rate

Negotiation is hard to avoid and can often shed light on whether this is a client that you really want to work with. If you are confident that your pricing reflects your value and the market rate, being haggled hard on price can get a relationship off on the wrong foot. Likewise, being locked in at a low rate can quickly devalue the relationship from your perspective.

So, when it comes to negotiating, be prepared to stand your ground but be willing to compromise. If you foresee further business here, try to be flexible. For example, could you deliver a one-page white paper, instead of two or cut back on the review cycles?

5. What About Retainers?

If a client starts to send a lot of volume your way, retainer-based pricing can be advantageous, even if it's at a lower hourly rate than your advertised price.

A retainer is a fee paid for a pre-determined amount of time or work (usually within a month) and is often paid up-front. A retainer agreement can deliver the benefit of predictable work and income while giving your client the reassurance of having you on "stand-by" and a clear view of monthly costs.

Many consultants charge the full retainer fee, even if they don't work the entire hours allocated. If you value the relationship, steer clear of this; instead, roll unused hours over to next month.

www.ingramcontent.com/pod-product-compliance
Lightning Source LLC
Chambersburg PA
CBHW072311170526
45158CB00003BA/1275